# 50 Top Tips for Well-Being

## Being

Creating a culture of well-being

in and away from work

~~~

Laura Henry

# About the author

Laura Henry is an expert, international award-winning Early Childhood specialist. She is the vice-president of The British Association for Early Childhood Education, an educational consultant for the BBC and Penguin Random House, and an ambassador for the Jermain Defoe Foundation.

For three decades, Laura has used her skills to support those who work directly with children. Every year, she trains thousands of individuals using her engaging and inspiring style and is highly regarded as a trainer and writer. She is passionate about quality in Early Childhood, making sure that children receive the best possible care and education to help them reach their full potential.

Laura regularly contributes to education and parenting publications. She has been a judge for GESS, TES, Nursery World and Nursery Management Today awards. She has used her specialist knowledge to work with government departments worldwide as well as national and international organisations, forums and working parties.

Laura's popular children's books 'Jo-Jo and Gran-Gran' have been commissioned by the BBC.

*"No one belongs here more than you."*

~ Brené Brown

# Introduction

Over the last few years, I've tried to take more responsibility for my own health and well-being. At times it hasn't been easy, but I know that it's essential to prevent problems further down the line.

In this book, I hope to share a range of tips and solutions that have helped me. They should be useful particularly for those who work with children – helping educators to maintain an emotional, mental, physical and spiritual balance.

My tips range from having a well-being charter to helping staff look after themselves when they are away from work.

I am delighted to partner with Ceeda, a leading provider of independent research and intelligence for childcare providers, investors, local authorities and sector stakeholders. Ceeda have worked with the sector for two decades, they are trusted to deliver insight and analysis that puts evidence at the heart of decision-making.

While the health of the individual is obviously of key importance, poor staff well-being can have other effects on a business.

The Department of Health's 2019 guidance, Health matters: health and work, includes the following statistics from Public Health England:

- 131 million working days are lost to sickness absences every year
- 34.3 million days are lost to minor illness
- 28.2 million days are lost to musculoskeletal conditions
- 14.3 million days are lost to stress

To access the full guidance, see further reading.

Clearly, these statistics should prompt us to ensure that we have a positive and impactful well-being culture within the workplace.

In its new Framework, Ofsted, the regulatory body in the UK for educational settings, schools and institutions, has stated clearly its expectations of how leaders must support staff:

*"Staff consistently report high levels of support for well-being issues."*

*"Leaders engage with their staff and are aware of the main pressures on them. They are realistic and constructive in the way they manage staff, including their workload."*

*"Leaders protect staff from harassment, bullying and discrimination."*

It's important to remember, as always, that we shouldn't be making improvements just for Ofsted, but should be doing what's right for the staff and children in our care, because this is what defines our setting's values.

This book is not a medical guide, and I'm not going to tell you what you do. I hope, though, that it's a gentle reminder of things you may already know and some extra useful advice and guidance.  More importantly, you know your own body, mind and soul.

These top tips are for everyone – use and adapt them in different situations, in work and within your personal life.

As we've seen, studies tell us that many sick days are taken due to stress-related illness.

As a leader, management of stress and well-being will be essential in your role supporting your team to be healthy in all areas of their life.

It's important to support your staff within the workplace. However, it is not your role to offer counselling or psychological guidance even if you have a qualification in this area; you could be creating a potential conflict of interest that could make a situation worse. Always signpost staff to their doctor or a reputable organisation that may be able to offer appropriate advice, guidance or support – there's a useful list at the end of this book.

Setting leaders need to be mindful that there may be staff who are suffering from posttraumatic stress or other mental health issues. It's good practice to encourage staff to be honest with you about anything that may prevent them from effectively carrying out their duties, and any triggers that you may need to be aware of. See the tip on one-page profiles. It is imperative that you take a non-judgemental and supportive stance. More on this later.

*"The time is always right to do what is right."*

~ Dr Martin Luther King Jr

# Getting started

## 1. Setting ethos

Any concept introduced within the
workplace needs to mirror your
setting's ethos. If you haven't got an
ethos in place, it's a good time to
consider what this should be. It
shouldn't only be written down; your
setting's ethos should be mirrored and
modelled in practice. Involve everyone

in shaping your ethos. It may be helpful to reflect on what you do as a setting, what you attach importance to, and how you involve children, parents, the environment and each other as a staff team.

## 2. Organisational behaviour and culture

Ideally, this should be included in the setting's ethos. This is where, as an organisation and team, you reflect on the meaning of your philosophy, expectations and way forward. Link back to your ethos and outline behaviours that need to be in place to keep everyone safe and what those behaviours look like to others outside your setting. This is how you interact with each other and how this is expressed. Similarly, explore how you get 'buy in' from all staff and parents on the setting's shared beliefs and attitudes.

## 3. Well-being charter

Once you've considered you ethos, you might want to consider a well-being charter, which should be a direct link to the setting's ethos. This will be the commitment to the well-being culture within your setting. I always like to keep written statements short; your charter should ideally take up no more than one page. You may want to mirror Ofsted's stance of intend, implement and impact when reflecting on your charter.

*Intend:*

- As a setting, what is important to you in terms of your well-being culture?

- Who is responsible and what is their role?

- What are you doing to support well-being within your setting?

- Why is well-being important within your setting?

- When and where does the promotion of well-being happen?


*Implement:*

- In practice, what are the activities and resources that are used to promote well-being within your setting?

*Impact:*

- What is the impact of your well-being charter? For example, a reduction in sick leave, staff feel supported, all members of the staff team embrace well-being and know it is a high priority.

*"For everyone, well-being is a journey. The secret is committing to that journey and taking those first steps with hope and belief in yourself."*

~ Deepak Chopra

## 4. Well-being ambassador

Having a lead person responsible for well-being sets the tone and demonstrates that you take well-being seriously. Rather than offering an existing member of staff the role, it's good practice to create a job description and person specification and carry out the recruitment process so that you demonstrate a transparent and robust approach. When creating the post, the senior leadership team should reflect on the setting's well-being charter and organisation's ethos. For example, leading on well-being events, sourcing and sharing relevant literature.

## 5. One-page profile

This is an excellent tool for leaders to support staff in a person-centred approach and offer personalised support. On a one-page sheet, staff can make a note of their needs, others can state what they admire about them and how leaders and colleagues can best support them in the team. One-page profiles are extremely helpful for leaders to effectively plan for meetings with staff. See the link in useful organisations below to Helen Sanderson, who explains in detail the one-page profile concept and provides a number of examples that you can use.

## 6. One-on-one meetings (supervision and appraisals)

It is essential to hold regular meetings that offer staff a safe place to share issues that may be affecting their health, well-being and welfare both at and outside work. Staff should know that these meetings are confidential and are a place where they feel supported and know that any issues or concerns they have will be acted upon, or that they will be signposted to an individual or organisation that can help.

## 7. Team meetings

These are an important part of any organisation. How often they take place should depend on what needs to be discussed and actioned. I believe that quality is better than quantity. The Teacher Tool Kit includes a five-minute meeting template, which is useful for keeping meetings brief and on track. See the link in useful organisations.

## 8. Walking meetings

These are a great way to gently exercise while talking at the same time and support the benefits of being outdoors and getting fresh air.

## 9. Induction

Make sure that the induction process mirrors your setting's well-being approach and staff are not overwhelmed within their first few weeks. Give new information in a way that supports how they learn and involve other staff in the process.

*"A group becomes a team when each member is sure enough of himself... to praise the skills of others."*

~ Norman Shidle

## 10. Coaching and mentoring

Include this in the induction process. Consider asking an existing member of staff to be a coach or mentor or you could bring in someone from outside. This could be another layer to how you support your staff.

## 11. Continuous professional development

Leaders need to keep a watchful eye on the amount of professional development staff are taking. Is it having a negative impact on the staff member's well-being? Are they finding any elements difficult? How do you assess the impact of continuous professional development – is this gathered by observation of practice, meetings, etc.?

## 12. Invited speakers

Within a staff meeting or an away day, invite in speakers that link to your well-being approach. For instance, this could be a nutritionist, personal trainer or an expert sharing tips on health, well-being and exercise.

## 13. Development/Business plan

How is staff well-being considered within the setting's development or business plan in terms of resources, time and budgets? Ensure leaders include a section on well-being within these important plans.

## 14. No gossiping

This signals a strong link back to the setting's ethos and organisational culture. Under no circumstances should gossip be tolerated. This should be discussed during the recruitment process and should include a definition of what gossiping is and how harmful it can be.

*"Gossip dies when it hits a wise person's ears."*

*~Source unknown*

## 15. No bullying

Under no circumstances should bullying, by a group or an individual, be tolerated. There must be an anti-bullying policy in place that states that staff should feel safe at work and should include procedures that will be robustly followed if bullying takes place.

## 16. Transparency

Being transparent is linked to the ethos and organisational behaviour of your setting – creating an environment where staff can be honest with each other. For instance, staff must be able to reflect on an incident and feel safe to state what went wrong and the lessons learnt without judgement from colleagues and leaders.

## 17. Breaks

Working with children is without doubt mentally and physically exhausting. It is important that staff have at least one break each day (this is a legal requirement) where they are away from children. In some settings, where staff may work up to 10 hours in a day, leaders have added a short break in the morning and afternoon.

## 18. Exercise clubs

These promote fitness within the setting and could be before the setting opens or closes and/or at lunch time. Clubs could be for any type of exercise that you decide on as a team, for example, running, yoga, stretching, etc. Exercise is a great way to release the endorphins that trigger positive feelings.

## 19. Healthy eating

Not only must healthy eating be promoted for children, it's a must for staff as well. Leaders should set the tone for healthy eating. Do you provide healthy snacks and meals for your staff, for instance a bowl of fruit or a healthy breakfast before they start? Do you have a no energy drinks or junk food policy in your setting? Even though staff may not eat with the children, a healthy eating culture needs a 360° approach.

## 20. Staff survey

It's important to understand how your staff members feel and to ascertain their views on how the setting is led and operates. Positive comments and expressions of concern should be given equal consideration when looking at results. Ceeda has created a robust and impactful staff survey for this purpose.

## 21. Treatments

Connect with a local college or training centre that offers training in alternative medicine and holistic health. It could be that you point your staff to them or their students come to you. Some establishments do this for free and for others there is a small charge.

## 22. Employee assistance programme

Depending on the size of your setting and your budget, you may want to sign up to one of these schemes. Some offer round-the-clock telephone and/or online support in areas such as legal issues and health. It's worth noting that if you're with a membership organisation, they may include this as part of their membership package.

## 23. Electronic communication and social media boundaries

We use a range of platforms to communicate with staff and parents – emails, Facebook and WhatsApp, for example. To protect your time, it's important to maintain a strict timeframe for this. For instance, some settings adopt a period between 7pm and 7am weekdays, weekends and holidays, when there will be no work or electronic communication and social media posting or sharing. This should be enforced and respected by all staff members and stakeholders.

## 24. Staff room/well-being zone

Ideally, the staff room should be an extension of your setting's environment. Discussions on how this should look and feel should be a staff decision, from offering healthy snacks as mentioned above, to comfortable seats, a professional development area, useful journals, books, flowers or plants, inspiring quotes or fragranced oils (being mindful of allergies).

*"A caring environment is a learning environment."*

~ Laura Henry

## 25. Share a meal:

This could be just with the staff or include parents and stakeholders. Consider an annual barbecue or link an event to a festival or celebration. Ask everyone to bring a dish that reflects their culture or even just a family favourite.

## 26. Birthdays

Agree as a team how staff birthdays are celebrated. Some staff may not want a 'fuss' while others may want their birthday to be acknowledged. For consistency and fairness, you could decide as a team how everyone contributes towards any gift for each staff member.

## 27. Festivals and celebrations

Festivals and celebrations could link to your community or what staff celebrate or acknowledge. Additionally, as a setting, build on your children's cultural experiences. Some settings decide annually as a team how they are going to celebrate.

## 28. Team away days

This doesn't have to link to a professional development goal and could just be a fun activity such as bike riding, attending a healthy eating workshop or a yoga retreat.

## 29. Notebooks/diary

Provide a notebook or diary for staff to make notes and to write their own personal reflections.

## 30. Discounts

Investigate whether there are any healthy eating places, gyms or leisure centres locally that may offer discounts to your staff. These might include trials and money off certain packages and food.

## 31. Vouchers

Budget permitting, consider offering a range of vouchers, for instance, a spa day or money off items. You may wish to link it to, for instance, long service or a member of staff passing an exam or achieving a qualification.

## 32. Growing vegetables and fruit

Do you have any land attached to your setting? If not, you may want to make an enquiry via your local authority about renting an allotment, or speak to a local land owner. This is a fantastic way to embrace the soil-to-table approach.

## 33. Local walks

Why not devise a few different walking routes within your locality, laminate them and let staff choose which route to take.

## 34. Reduce your carbon footprint

Encourage, where possible, staff to walk or cycle to and from work. If staff use public transport, maybe suggest that once or twice a week they get off at the stop before and walk the rest of the way. If staff must drive, can they leave their car at home for one day during the week or month?

*"Do the best you can until you know better. Then when you know better, do better."*

~ Maya Angelou

## 35.  Smoke-free zone

Smoking, as we know, is illegal within settings. It's a fact, though, that some staff do smoke and are aware of the negative impact that smoking can have on an individual's short, medium and long-term health. Leaders can provide literature to staff who wish to stop smoking and point them to agencies that can help and support them.

## 36.  Holidays

It's essential that leaders make sure that staff take their holiday entitlement and any time in lieu that is owed to them. There should be a general agreement that staff are not contacted while on leave. There may be an exception to this rule, and a setting would need to decide collectively when and how this is done. If there are solid systems in place and an effective paper trail of information this should not happen.

## 37. Extra hours

There may be times when staff must work extra hours; staff meetings, parent meetings, out-of-hours training. This needs to be written clearly in their contracts and expectations explained.

The setting leader should take a stance on how long staff should be in the building before, after work and at weekends. If staff are doing this regularly, questions should be asked as to what they are doing and why it is important. Consider setting times when the building will open and close and reiterate that this is linked to your setting's well-being ethos.

## 38. Workload

Leaders should keep a watchful eye on staff workload and ask relevant questions during meetings. Most paperwork is not necessary and leaders may need to reflect on what is essential. Equally, staff should not be taking work home. The EYFS reminds us that paperwork should be kept to a minimum, however, if paperwork needs completing, for instance reports, leaders should give staff time away from the children during the working day.

## 39. Keep hydrated

Make sure that water is available and that staff are encouraged to drink it regularly. In staff communal areas, offer sugar-free juices, herbal teas and decaffeinated coffee and tea.

## 40. Extra day a year

Although it will depend on many factors, consider offering staff one extra day's holiday a year. They could use this for a celebration or festival. Of course, this would need to be coordinated in line with the needs of the setting.

## 41. Hobbies/interests

Having a hobby or interest outside work is a great way to switch off. This could be a dance class or a theatre visit, for example. Leaders could encourage staff to share their hobbies within meetings.

*"Don't wait. The time will never be just right."*

~ Napoleon Hill

## 42. Health checks

Most doctors do a free health check, and it may be useful for leaders to remind staff about this on an annual basis.

## 43. Cheap treats

An Epsom salt and lavender bath can aid relaxation. Please note that some people can be allergic to these products.

Add two cups of Epsom salt and a couple of drops of lavender oil to running warm water and relax away with some me time. Investigate meditation and relaxation apps – there are lots that you can download and listen to at home.

## 44. Involve parents

Support setting-to-home links and vice versa. Inform parents about your well-being stance as a setting and why this is important. Organise joint parents and staff well-being activities and share suggestions.

## 45. Social media breaks

You may want to consider switching off from social media to give your mind a break from the constant information that comes in. This could be one day a week or month, or one dedicated evening.

## 46. Family and friends

Be sure to make time to connect with your family and friends. Having a meal or going out socialising can help make sure that your work-life balance is in check.

## 47. Online discount vouchers

There are lots that you can sign up to in order to receive emails or you can install a company's app. They often offer heavy discounts on a range of treats, services and equipment that can support your well-being.

## 48. Short breaks

It's sometimes easier to have a short holiday for two to three days rather than two weeks. There are some good deals to be had either in advance or last minute. Consider a 'staycation' instead of an overseas break.

## 49. Eat healthily

In our busy lifestyles, cooking can become a chore, encouraging us to eat overly processed food, which can have a negative impact on our body. Download free recipes that are healthy, cost effective and quick to make. Try cooking in bulk and freezing for later. Remember that frozen vegetables are just as good as fresh.

## 50. Ask for help

If, at any time, you feel overwhelmed, anxious or stressed it's important that you reach out to your line manager, family, friend or a professional organisation who can offer appropriate help and guidance.

*"No matter who you are, no matter where you come from, you are beautiful."*

~ Michelle Obama

# Useful organisations

**Acas:** www.acas.org.uk

Free and impartial information and advice to employers and employees on all aspects of workplace relations and employment law

**Action Amanda:**

www.amandasactionclub.co.uk

Weekly sessions to promote the importance of exercise and fitness to the under-fives and their families.

**Ceeda:** www.ceeda.co.uk

Designed by experts to keep you in touch with staff views and experience. Use

EYsurveys to understand and support staff well-being, motivation and retention.

**Helen Sanderson:**
www.helensandersonassociates.co.uk
Bespoke training promoting a person-centred approach

**Jane Evans:** www.thejaneevans.com
Life change and parenting coach

**Kate Moxley:** www.katemoxleyeyc.co.uk
Early Years consultant specialising in mental health and well-being

**Mind:** www.mind.org.uk
Mental health support charity

**NHS**: www.nhs.uk

Stop smoking advice and other useful information

**Samaritans:** www.samaritans.org

Charity dedicated to reducing feelings of isolation and disconnection that can lead to suicide

**Sane:** www.sane.org.uk

Mental health support charity

**Sue Atkins:** sueatkinsparentingcoach.com

Parenting coach and online community

**Teacher Toolkit:**

www.teachertoolkit.co.uk/5minplan/series

A range of free resources for educators

**Young Minds:** www.youngminds.org.uk

Youth mental health support

# Further reading

- Identity and the Modern Organization – Caroline A. Bartel, Steven Blader, Amy Wrzesniewski
- Dare to Lead – Brené Brown
- Health matters: health and work – Department of Heath

# Other books by the author

- Jo-Jo and Gran-Gran, All in a Week
- Jo-Jo and Gran-Gran, 12 ½ Days of Christmas
- A to Z of Inspiring Early Years: Paragraphs
- Play Foundations – Senses (co-authored with Jeanette Phillips-Green)
- Laura's Rhymes

# Consultancy and training

Please email:

Laura@LauraHenryConsultancy.com

jov@ceeda.co.uk

## Connect on social media:

Twitter: @IamLauraHenry @ceeda_UK

Facebook: @LauraHenryConsultancy

@Ceeda-Research-Limited

Instagram: @LauraHenryConsultancy

ISBN: **9781687349637**

28042832R00036

Printed in Great Britain
by Amazon